AID

AUTISM INVENTORY OF DEVELOPMENT™

Roya Ostovar, Ph.D.

An Assessment Tool for Parents and Professionals

Your name: _____ Relationship to the child: _____ Date: _____

Child's name: _____ Sex: ❑ Female ❑ Male Date of birth: _____

Age: _____ Current grade in school: _____

Handedness: ❑ Right ❑ Left ❑ Ambidextrous (no preference)

AUTISM INVENTORY OF DEVELOPMENT™

All marketing and publishing rights guaranteed to and reserved by:

FUTURE HORIZONS INC.

721 W. Abram Street
Arlington, TX 76013
(800) 489-0727
(817) 277-0727
(817) 277-2270 (fax)
E-mail: info@fhautism.com
www.fhautism.com

ISBN: 9781941765784

INTRODUCTION

The Autism Inventory Development (AID) was designed to be a tool to gather critical information for the process of assessing for Autism Spectrum Disorder. Autism is classified within the category of "Neurodevelopmental Disorders" by the Diagnostic and Statistical Manual of Mental Disorders, DSM-5. The diagnoses included in this category are characterized by having a certain combination of social, emotional, and behavioral symptoms apparent before the child enters elementary school. As part of a thorough and accurate evaluation, an extensive developmental history must be obtained. Usually the AID is completed by parents, caregivers, or family members who are rather familiar with the individual's childhood starting at a young age.

The critical informational areas the AID covers include the following:

- Family History
- Child History
- Medical History
- Developmental Milestones
- Communication

- Cognitive and Executive Functioning Abilities
- Social Functioning
- Interests
- Sensory Integration and Processing
- Behaviors

The types of questions within each of these categories were designed to obtain very specific pieces of information that can be helpful for diagnostic purposes. Many of the questions allow the individual completing the form to expand upon and give further descriptions of the child's development. Testing alone will not reveal the type of necessary information needed to make an accurate diagnosis.

The AID was created with two purposes in mind. First, it was created for clinicians to obtain a comprehensive record of a child's history to assist in the diagnostic process. Second, and equally important, it was created for parents, caregivers, and/or family members to create a record for themselves that holds critical and important historical information for the individual being assessed.

INSTRUCTIONS

- Please read and answer all of the following questions regarding your child's or adult child's development to the best of your ability and recollection.

- Provide as much information as you can. Unless otherwise noted, please answer questions that reflect your child's skills prior to the age of 18.

- If you cannot remember or do not have certain information, skip that question and continue on with the next question.

- Once you complete the form, please return it to the clinician that you are working with.

Current Prescription Medications: _____

_____

_____

Current Mental Health Diagnosis (if any): _____

_____

_____

Behavioral Concerns: _____

_____

_____

Diet restrictions: _____

_____

_____

FAMILY HISTORY

MATERNAL HISTORY

Is there any history of ...

Learning Disorders	❑ No	❑ Yes
If yes, what and whom?_____		
Psychiatric Disorders	❑ No	❑ Yes
If yes, what and whom?_____		
Intellectual Disability	❑ No	❑ Yes
If yes, what and whom?_____		
Autism Spectrum Disorder	❑ No	❑ Yes
If yes, what and whom?_____		
Genetic syndromes or chromosomal abnormalities	❑ No	❑ Yes
If yes, what and whom?_____		

Other: _____

_____

PATERNAL HISTORY

Is there any history of ...

Learning Disorders   ❑ No   ❑ Yes

    If yes, what and whom?_____

Psychiatric Disorders   ❑ No   ❑ Yes

    If yes, what and whom?_____

Intellectual Disability   ❑ No   ❑ Yes

    If yes, what and whom?_____

Autism Spectrum Disorder   ❑ No   ❑ Yes

    If yes, what and whom?_____

Genetic syndromes or chromosomal abnormalities   ❑ No   ❑ Yes

    If yes, what and whom?_____

Other: _____

_____

SIBLING HISTORY

List child's sibling history of learning disorders, psychiatric disorders, intellectual disability, or other significant conditions:

_____

_____

_____

_____

_____

Autism Inventory of Development™

CHILD HISTORY (Perinatal through Early Development)

PERINATAL HISTORY

This child is ❏ Adopted ❏ Foster Child ❏ Biological Other: _____

Total number of pregnancies: _____ Number of live births: _____ Birth order of this baby: _____

Mother's age during pregnancy: _____

Was the pregnancy healthy? ❏ No ❏ Yes

During pregnancy, did the child's mother:

Use drugs? ❏ No ❏ Yes If yes, what kind? _____
How much/how often? _____

Use prescribed medications? ❏ No ❏ Yes If yes, what kind? _____
How much/how often? _____

Use alcohol? ❏ No ❏ Yes If yes, what kind? _____
How much/how often? _____

Drink caffeine? ❏ No ❏ Yes If yes, what kind? _____
How much/how often? _____

Smoke? ❏ No ❏ Yes If yes, what kind? _____
How much/how often? _____

Have a fever? ❏ No ❏ Yes If yes, how high and for how long?_____

Have high blood pressure? ❏ No ❏ Yes If yes, how high and for how long?_____

Get hurt, injured seriously, or hospitalized? ❏ No ❏ Yes If yes, how? _____

Have diabetes? ❏ No ❏ Yes

Have toxemia? (Pregnancy induced hypertension) ❏ No ❏ Yes

Have eclampsia? (a toxic condition characterized by convulsions in those with high blood pressure) ❏ No ❏ Yes

DELIVERY HISTORY

Was the pregnancy: ❑ Full term   ❑ Premature (at what week was your child born? _____)

How long was labor? _____

Check all that apply regarding labor with this child:

❑ Normal

❑ Spontaneous

❑ Induced

❑ Induced with Pitocin (synthetic hormone to start contraction)

❑ Emergency   If emergency, why? _____

❑ Scheduled   If scheduled, why? _____

❑ Breech (feet first)

❑ Caesarian Section

❑ Anesthesia (If yes, what type? _____)

❑ Meconium stained amniotic fluid delivery

NEWBORN HISTORY (FIRST MONTH)

What was your child's: Apgar Score (at 1 minute): _____   Birth Weight: _____

Did or was your child:

Have any birth injuries?	❑ No	❑ Yes	If yes, describe: _____ _____
Have trouble starting to breathe?	❑ No	❑ Yes	If yes, for how long? _____
Need oxygen?	❑ No	❑ Yes	If yes, for how long? _____
Born with the cord around his/her neck?	❑ No	❑ Yes	
Jaundiced?	❑ No	❑ Yes	If yes, for how long? _____
Anemic?	❑ No	❑ Yes	If yes, describe: _____ _____

NEWBORN HISTORY (FIRST MONTH) CONTINUED

Require transfusions?	❏ No	❏ Yes	If yes, for how much?_____
Born with birth defects?	❏ No	❏ Yes	If yes, with what? _____
A twin?	❏ No	❏ Yes	
Hospitalized more than five days?	❏ No	❏ Yes	If yes, why? _____
Have trouble sucking?	❏ No	❏ Yes	If yes, for how long? _____
Have trouble with gagging reflux or vomiting?	❏ No	❏ Yes	If yes, describe: _____ _____
Have seizures?	❏ No	❏ Yes	If yes, describe: _____ _____
Have other problems not noted, above (sepsis, meningitis, high fever)?	❏ No	❏ Yes	If yes, describe: _____ _____

EARLY DEVELOPMENTAL HISTORY

Was your child breastfed?	❏ No	❏ Yes	If yes, for how long?_____

Does or did your child have difficulty with any of the following:

❏ Sucking reflex

❏ Weight gain

❏ Sleeping habits

❏ Eating habits

❏ Responses to mother's cues

❏ Startle reaction

❏ Other: _____

How would you describe your child's temperament within first two years of life:

❏ Easy   ❏ Slow to Warm Up   ❏ Difficult   ❏ Other: _____

Reminder: For adult children, unless otherwise noted, rate the following to reflect your child's abilities prior to the age of 18

DEVELOPMENTAL MILESTONES

EARLY GROSS MOTOR SKILLS

Describe your child's early gross motor activity, such as balance and movement:

❏ Normal   ❏ Clumsy   ❏ Robotic   ❏ Other: _____

Approximately at what age did your child first:

Roll over: _____   Sit up independently: _____   Crawl: _____   Walk independently: _____

At what age did your child learn to ride a bicycle independently? _____

If child was over the age of 6, explain. _____

_____

Does or did your child have difficulty with any of the following tasks:

❏ Hopping on one foot

❏ Climbing on play structures

❏ Walking up and down stairs

❏ Jumping over objects

❏ Running with changing directions

❏ Other: _____

List anything unusual about your child's early gross motor activity, such as balance and movement:

_____

_____

EARLY FINE MOTOR SKILLS

Describe your child's early fine motor ability, such as hand movements:

❑ Normal ❑ Adequate ❑ Poor ❑ Other: _____

Does or did your child have difficulty with any of the following tasks:

❑ Building three-dimensional structures using blocks

❑ Using scissors to cut paper

❑ Completing puzzles

❑ Weak grasp

❑ Holding a pencil to draw or write

❑ Using electronics (e.g., typing, video games)

❑ Other _____

MUSCLE STRENGTH & ENERGY LEVEL

Does or did your child have difficulty with any of the following:

❑ Low muscle tone

❑ Poor endurance

❑ Getting tired easily

❑ Poor body strength to lift or lower self

❑ Needing help with body support when seated or standing (e.g., head on desk, leaning on the wall)

❑ Other _____

Reminder: For adult children, unless otherwise noted, rate the following to reflect your child's abilities prior to the age of 18

SPEECH, COMMUNICATION, LANGUAGE

Does or did your child have speech problems or misarticulations? ❑ No ❑ Yes

If yes, explain. _____

_____

Did your child have a speech and language evaluation? ❑ No ❑ Yes

If yes, at what age? _____

If yes, what was the result of the speech and language evaluation? _____

_____

Does or did your child have difficulty with any of the following:

❑ Smiling at 4-6 weeks

❑ Cooing at 3 months

❑ Babbling at 6 months

❑ Jargon at 10 to 14 months

❑ First word at 12 months (What was your child's first word? _____

❑ Three words at 12 months (other than Mama or Dada)

   List words other than Mama or Dada: _____

❑ Two-word combinations at 22 months

❑ Three-word combinations at 3 years

❑ Other _____

Describe your child's speech rhythm:

❑ Normal   ❑ Slow   ❑ Rapid/pressured   ❑ Other: _____

Describe your child's speech inflection (i.e., tone, pitch, volume, and/or emphasis of speech):

❑ Normal   ❑ Flat   ❑ Monotonous   ❑ Pedantic   ❑ Other: _____

REGRESSIONS

Regression means to have had a skill and then losing the skill. For example, being able to use complete sentences, then only using single words or being able to walk, then only crawling.

Did your child ever develop a skill and then regress, lose the skill, and could not do it again? ❑ No ❑ Yes

If yes, explain. _____

_____

COMMUNICATION

QUALITY OF LANGUAGE & CONVERSATION

Does or did your child's conversation or language style include:

Lack of cohesion in conversation?	❑ No	❑ Yes
Non-sequiturs? (starting a new topic before completing the first topic)	❑ No	❑ Yes
Idiosyncratic (odd) use of words/phrases?	❑ No	❑ Yes
Repetitive speech patterns or vocalizations?	❑ No	❑ Yes
Odd intonation or inappropriate pitch? (e.g., whispering)	❑ No	❑ Yes
Immediate Echolalia? (repeating words and phrases immediately after hearing the word or phrase)	❑ No	❑ Yes
Delayed Echolalia? (repeating words and phrases with a time lapse after hearing the word or phrase)	❑ No	❑ Yes
Spontaneous elaboration about his or her own thoughts, feelings, or experiences?	❑ No	❑ Yes
Mimicking?	❑ No	❑ Yes
Following a logical sequence in conversation?	❑ No	❑ Yes
Rapid digression from one idea to the next?	❑ No	❑ Yes
Loose associations or was difficult to follow in conversation?	❑ No	❑ Yes
Conversations with others on topics of mutual interest?	❑ No	❑ Yes
Initiation of conversations on topics that were of interest to peers?	❑ No	❑ Yes
Laughing or smiling appropriately in response to peers?	❑ No	❑ Yes
Reciprocal conversation, such as asking others about their thoughts, feelings or experiences?	❑ No	❑ Yes

❑ Other _____

Reminder: For adult children, unless otherwise noted, rate the following to reflect your child's abilities prior to the age of 18

Autism Inventory of Development™

NONVERBAL COMMUNICATION

Does or did your child have difficulty with the following:

- ❑ Interpreting facial expressions
- ❑ Reading emotion from facial expressions
- ❑ Using facial expressions
- ❑ Making eye contact
- ❑ Staring
- ❑ Using hand gestures
- ❑ Awareness of own body space
- ❑ Coming too close to others
- ❑ Maintaining body posture
- ❑ Responding to nonverbal cues in conversation
- ❑ Other _____

Does or did your child use the following types of nonverbal communication?

- ❑ Descriptive (acting out an event or how to use an object, such as acting out how a plane flies)
- ❑ Conventional (e.g., thumbs up for "good job")
- ❑ Instrumental (e.g., pointing, shrugging, head-nodding)
- ❑ Emphatical (providing emphasis to what is being said, such as covering the mouth for surprise)

Does or did your child use eye contact, facial expressions, or gestures appropriately while speaking?　❑ No　❑ Yes

Is your child able to use facial expressions or gestures to communicate affective (e.g., surprise, disgust)　❑ No　❑ Yes

or cognitive (e.g., skepticism, confusion) states?

Do you suspect your child could read facial expressions and use body language or do you feel he or she has a deficit in this ability? Explain. _____

_____

_____

UNDERSTANDING OF COMMUNICATION

Does or did your child have difficulty with the following:

- ☐ Nonliteral speech
- ☐ Irony
- ☐ Sarcasm
- ☐ Joking
- ☐ Metaphors
- ☐ Inferential communication (recognition of intent in communication)
- ☐ Other _____

Does your child ask for clarification if he or she is confused by any of these types of communication?   ☐ No   ☐ Yes

Describe your child's interpretation of language

☐ Normal   ☐ Literal   ☐ Rigid   ☐ Other _____

Reminder: For adult children, unless otherwise noted, rate the following to reflect your child's abilities prior to the age of 18

EXPRESSING EMOTIONS

Describe your child's understanding of emotions:

❑ Full understanding

❑ Difficulty with understanding range of emotions

❑ Only knows sad, happy, angry

❑ Other _____

Describe your child's affect (meaning the expression of his/her emotions):

❑ Full/Exaggerated expression

❑ Normal/Expected expression

❑ Limited or restricted expression

❑ Flat/Non-Expressive

❑ Unexpected/Inappropriate Expression (does not match the situation)

❑ Other _____

Describe how your child's affect changes:

❑ Smooth changes

❑ Fixed (affect rarely changes)

❑ Abrupt changes

❑ Other _____

Describe how your child communicates anger or frustration:

❑ Throwing things (not to hurt anybody), slamming doors

❑ Screaming, yelling, swearing

❑ Aggression toward self

❑ Aggression toward others (e.g., hitting, biting, verbal threats of physical harm)

❑ Other _____

Describe how your child communicates anxiety:

❑ Withdrawal/avoidance

❑ Physical signs (e.g., trembling, jumpy, sweating)

❑ Voicing worries or concerns

❑ Other _____

EXPRESSING EMOTIONS CONTINUED

Does or did your child treat people as objects?	❏ No	❏ Yes
Does or did your child notice when you, other adults, or peers were feeling happy, sad, angry, etc?	❏ No	❏ Yes
Does or did your child seem to "live in his or her own world"?	❏ No	❏ Yes
Did your child have a snuggly object after age 6?	❏ No	❏ Yes
Does your child's emotional reaction seem disproportionate to the situation?	❏ No	❏ Yes
Was your child able to communicate emotions verbally?	❏ No	❏ Yes
To understand how your child was feeling, did you have to rely on his or her behaviors to show you?	❏ No	❏ Yes

Reminder: For adult children, unless otherwise noted, rate the following to reflect your child's abilities prior to the age of 18

COGNITIVE & EXECUTIVE FUNCTIONING ABILITES

Does or did your child:

Understand relevant from non-relevant information? (able to judge what parts of a task or conversation are important to note and which can be ignored) ❑ No ❑ Yes

Do well with details? ❑ No ❑ Yes

See the whole picture and understand the main idea? ❑ No ❑ Yes

Understand cause and effect? ❑ No ❑ Yes

Demonstrate ability to generate alternative solutions to problems? ❑ No ❑ Yes

Understand consequential thinking? ❑ No ❑ Yes

Demonstrate flexibility in his/her thinking and to change his/her mind easily and as needed? ❑ No ❑ Yes

Have rigid and inflexible thinking? ❑ No ❑ Yes

Learn from past experiences? ❑ No ❑ Yes

Demonstrate ability to shift and move on from one subject to another with ease? ❑ No ❑ Yes

Have impulse control? ❑ No ❑ Yes

❑ Other _____

How does your child respond to being asked to return back to a task or change to a different task?

_____

SOCIAL FUNCTIONING

Check all that apply to your child for childhood (under the age of 12):

Took care of personal needs (e.g., personal hygiene) ❑ No ❑ Yes If no, describe: _____

Had close friends ❑ No ❑ Yes If no, describe: _____

Avoided others ❑ No ❑ Yes If yes, describe: _____

Was interested in peers/friends ❑ No ❑ Yes If no, describe: _____

Wanted desperately to interact with peers ❑ No ❑ Yes If no, describe: _____

Check all that apply to your child recently (including adult children's most recent presentation):

Takes care of personal needs (e.g., personal hygiene) ❑ No ❑ Yes If no, describe: _____

Has close friends ❑ No ❑ Yes If no, describe: _____

Avoids others ❑ No ❑ Yes If yes, describe: _____

Interested in peers/friends ❑ No ❑ Yes If yes, describe: _____

Wants desperately to interact with peers ❑ No ❑ Yes If yes, describe: _____

Does your child currently have the following skills?

Greets others in an appropriate manner ❑ No ❑ Yes If no, describe: _____

Initiates conversations ❑ No ❑ Yes If no, describe: _____

Continues conversations ❑ No ❑ Yes If no, describe: _____

Reminder: For adult children, unless otherwise noted, rate the following to reflect your child's abilities prior to the age of 18

Reads cues to enter social groups	❑ No	❑ Yes	If no, describe: _____
			_____
Ends conversations appropriately	❑ No	❑ Yes	If no, describe: _____
			_____

Does or did your child:

Respond to his/her name being called within the first or second call? (e.g., with eye contact or verbal response)	❑ No	❑ Yes	If no, describe: _____ _____
Usually share and take turns willingly?	❑ No	❑ Yes	If no, describe: _____ _____
Usually play well with two or more children?	❑ No	❑ Yes	If no, describe: _____ _____
Willingly and cooperatively participate in small groups, activities, and/or games?	❑ No	❑ Yes	If no, describe: _____ _____
Play pretend games?	❑ No	❑ Yes	Describe: _____ _____
Have a one-sided response in conversations?	❑ No	❑ Yes	If yes, describe: _____ _____
Have difficulty understanding the feelings of others?	❑ No	❑ Yes	If yes, describe: _____ _____
Ever express being lonely?	❑ No	❑ Yes	If yes, describe: _____ _____
Know how to have informal chit-chat? (e.g., talk about the weather, polite conversation)	❑ No	❑ Yes	If yes, describe: _____ _____
Change behavior to match the environment or who they are talking to? (e.g., be formal in an interview, talk more simply when around younger children)	❑ No	❑ Yes	If yes, describe: _____ _____
Understand social cues?	❑ No	❑ Yes	If yes, describe: _____ _____
Prefer solitary activities?	❑ No	❑ Yes	If yes, describe: _____ _____

SOCIAL INTERACTIONS

Did your child have difficulty relating to you or other adults?	❑ No	❑ Yes
Did your child prefer to be in the company of adults compared to similar-aged peers?	❑ No	❑ Yes
Did your child have difficulty relating to similar-aged peers?	❑ No	❑ Yes
Did your child prefer to interact with younger or older children?	❑ No	❑ Yes
If your child needs something, will they ask you or another adult for assistance?	❑ No	❑ Yes
Does your child only interact with you or other adults to get their needs met (i.e., asking you	❑ No	❑ Yes
to do things for them)?	❑ No	❑ Yes
Can your child share an adult's attention?	❑ No	❑ Yes
Does your child start talking to others without getting their attention?	❑ No	❑ Yes
Does your child feel anxious in situations involving new people?	❑ No	❑ Yes
Is your child preoccupied with his or her own inner world?	❑ No	❑ Yes
Does (or did) your child engage in mutual sharing of interests, activities, or emotions?	❑ No	❑ Yes
Does your child appear to enjoy interacting with others?	❑ No	❑ Yes
Does your child understand what it means to be a friend?	❑ No	❑ Yes
Does your child understand what it means to be a partner in a romantic relationship?	❑ No	❑ Yes

Describe your child's need for your or other caregiver's attention:

❑ Unusually intense or excessive demands for attention

❑ Little concern paid towards having attention

❑ Frequent (typical) and spontaneous attempts to gain and/or maintain your attention

❑ Other: _____

Reminder: For adult children, unless otherwise noted, rate the following to reflect your child's abilities prior to the age of 18

INTERESTS

Describe your child's preschool play interests:

❑ Narrow   ❑ Restricted   ❑ Similar to peers the same age   ❑ Other: _____

Describe your child's play with peers in preschool:

❑ Parallel (beside)

❑ Cooperative

❑ Peripheral (distant, away from)

❑ Interactive with peers (with)

❑ Flexible

❑ Other: _____

Does or did your child have a preoccupation with the nonfunctional aspects of objects, such as:

❑ Odor

❑ Spinning objects

❑ Feeling of surfaces of objects

❑ Noise/Vibration of objects

❑ Other: _____

Does your child have any savant (exceptional) skills?	❑ No	❑ Yes
Explain: _____		
Does your child have rote memory for facts?	❑ No	❑ Yes
Explain: _____		
Does your child collect or save things?	❑ No	❑ Yes
Explain: _____		
Did or does your child have difficulty creating a make-believe story or creative thought?	❑ No	❑ Yes
Did or does the make-believe story or creative thought seem to be repetitive or reflect a preferred interest?	❑ No	❑ Yes
Did or does your child often make references to unusual or highly specific topics or interests that interfere with conversations?	❑ No	❑ Yes

Check any special interests or talents your child may have:

❑ Dinosaurs	❑ Electronics
❑ Maps	❑ Weapons
❑ Computers/Tablets	❑ Vehicles
❑ Weather	❑ Fans
❑ Video Games	❑ Railroad Systems/Cars

❑ Other: _____

Describe your child's range of interests:

❑ Normal

❑ Nonexistent (child doesn't like anything)

❑ Restricted to one interest (child seems obsessed by one area of interest)

❑ Restricted to one or two interests

❑ Other: _____

Check all that describe your child's PRESCHOOL use of toys:

❑ Sequenced, lined up	❑ Symbolic use
❑ Repetitive/Routine	❑ Spontaneous/Typical
❑ Preoccupation with parts of toys or objects	❑ Restrictive (continuous play with a specific object)

❑ Other: _____

When given free time or a break, how does your child occupy himself or herself?

_____

Reminder: For adult children, unless otherwise noted, rate the following to reflect your child's abilities prior to the age of 18

SENSORY INTEGRATION & PROCESSING

Does or did your child have sensory processing or sensory difficulties? ❏ No ❏ Yes

Explain: _____

Has your child ever received a diagnosis of Sensory Processing Disorder (SPD)? ❏ No ❏ Yes

Has your child ever been evaluated by an occupational therapist? ❏ No ❏ Yes

If yes, at what age? _____

If yes, what was the result of the evaluation? _____

Rate your child's reaction to the following:

Sense	Over-Responsive	Normal	Under-Responsive	Describe Problems
Touch (e.g., pulls away from hugs or being touched, doesn't like new clothes, prefers certain fabrics)	1	2	3	_____ _____ _____ _____
Sounds (e.g., unusual responses to loud noises, covers ears from sounds)	1	2	3	_____ _____ _____ _____
Smell (e.g., avoids certain smells, notices smells that are hardly recognizable to others)	1	2	3	_____ _____ _____ _____
Taste (e.g., will only eat certain foods, has limitations on particular food textures)	1	2	3	List preferred foods: _____ _____ _____ List avoided foods: _____ _____ _____
Visual Stimulus (e.g., bothered by bright lights that others adapt to, seemingly distracted by people moving around a room)	1	2	3	_____ _____ _____

Reminder: For adult children, unless otherwise noted, rate the following to reflect your child's abilities prior to the age of 18

BEHAVIORS

STEREOTYPED BEHAVIORS

Stereotyped behaviors are unusual repetitive and/or excessive body movements. Examples include odd finger or body movements, running in circles, staring at a fan, spinning objects, or lining objects or toys.

Did or does your child have "stereotypes" or stereotyped behaviors? ❑ No ❑ Yes

Does or did your child have any of the following:

❑ Hand/finger flapping ❑ Rocking

❑ Hand movements ❑ Sniffing materials

❑ Pacing ❑ Purposeless complex whole-body movements

❑ Head banging ❑ Other: _____

At what ages did the stereotyped behavior(s) begin and at what age did the behavior(s) stop? _____

_____

Did your child ever engage in self-injurious behaviors? ❑ No ❑ Yes

If yes, at what age? _____

Describe self-injurious behaviors _____

_____

Describe the response/treatment to these behaviors: _____

_____

_____

NEED FOR SAMENESS

Does or did your child have difficulty with any of the following:

❑ Transitions ❑ New situations

❑ Small changes in routines ❑ Unexpected change in schedule

❑ Small changes in details ❑ Other: _____

What was your child's response when any of the above occurred? _____

_____

RITUALS

Does or did your child have excessive repetitive fears, worries, or rituals? ❑ No ❑ Yes

When were they first noticed? _____

Have they stopped? ❑ No ❑ Yes

Describe the main fears/worries/obsessions: _____

_____

Describe the rituals/compulsions: _____

_____

What is/was your child's response if a ritual or routine was interrupted? _____

_____

MISCELLANEOUS

At what age of your child did you notice or feel there was something different about your child? Describe what you noticed.

_____

_____

_____

Describe any other delays, abnormalities, or concerns you may have in any areas of development not mentioned above:

_____

_____

_____

Also by Roya Ostovar

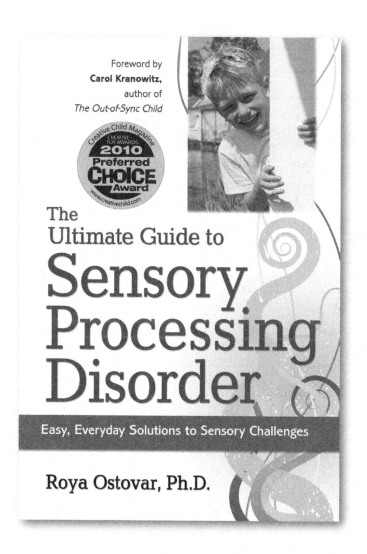

Foreword by **Carol Kranowitz**, author of *The Out-of-Sync Child*

CREATIVE TOY AWARDS 2010 Preferred CHOICE Award www.creativechild.com

The Ultimate Guide to **Sensory Processing Disorder**

Easy, Everyday Solutions to Sensory Challenges

Roya Ostovar, Ph.D.

From the author of *The Ultimate Guide to Sensory Processing Disorder*

5 things you need to know about **Social Skills Coaching**

Your Guide to Better Communication Skills in the Modern World

Roya Ostovar, PhD & Krista DiVittore, PsyD